# The Art Of Conversations

Jack Ricchiuto

DesigningLife Books

## Books by Jack Ricchiuto

*Collaborative Creativity* / 1996
*Accidental Conversations* / 2002
*Project Zen* / 2003
*Appreciative Leadership* / 2005
*Mountain Paths* / 2007
*Conscious Becoming* / 2008
*Instructions From The Cook* / 2009
*The Stories That Connect Us* / 2010
*The Enchantment Of Casual Origins* / 2011
*The Joy Of Thriving* / 2012
*Ordinary Eyes* / 2012
*The Agile Canvas Field Guide* / 2012
*Abundant Possibilities* / 2013
*The Power Of Circles* / 2013
*Making Sense Of Time* / 2014
*Beyond Recipes* / 2014
*Focus* / 2015
*Smarter Together* / 2015
*Ideas* / 2015
*The Art Of Conversations* / 2016

**The Art Of Conversations**

Published by DesigningLife Books
1020 Kenilworth Avenue
Cleveland OH 44113 USA

ISBN 978-1522978169
Paperback

1. Conversation. Social Connection. Relationships.
I. Title

Printed in the USA

Production: CreateSpace
Cover: Tia Andrako

# Content

## Conversation Primacy

## Conversation Essentials

**Connecting Conversations**

## Conversation Hacks

## Conversation Everyday

# Invitation

This is a conversation about conversations.

Conversation is life. Consider your life so far and all the learning and loving, succeeding and surviving, delighting and dreaming you have done in conversations.

We live in a world of unprecedented complexity, change and connectivity. Flourishing will happen because we know how to have connecting conversations. The heart of our optimism about creating a world that works is a palpable sense how new and connecting conversations make this possible.

We're concerned about losing the art of conversation. Conversation becomes a species at risk in a world when people sit silently with one another, busy somewhere else, through the ubiquity of small screens. Technology is changing our whole sensibilities about what it means to be in conversation.

This book is an invitation to become more vividly aware of the art of conversations. It is research rich, including a recent global study with 285 people. It draws from my last three decades working across the globe helping people in organizations and communities become more deeply connected and enjoy the fruits of the process.

It's practical, offering over 100 reflective questions and everyday practices to cultivate the art of conversations in every dimension of your life.

The book spans an array of topics including neuroscience, intimacy, last goodbyes, technology, meetings, humor, community, politics, religion, emotional connection and talking about anything with anybody. It focuses on personal, work and civic conversational contexts.

It has unique value when read together by people who regularly share conversations. It will inspire new sensitives and possibilities as never before.

It's now becoming more apparent than ever that the possibility of our personal and collective flourishing is equal to the quality of our conversations. Let's take this path together.


Jack Ricchiuto
January 15, 2016

# Conversation Primacy

## In The Beginning

In the beginning is the conversation.

Everything we know as human, everything loved and loathed, began in conversation. When youngsters ask us where babies come from, we accurately say it's likely they begin in conversations.

When things go well in our lives and relationships, in our work and world, it's because of the quality of conversations that brought them about.

At the root of things not going well are conversations that don't go well. All the violence we daily see, hear and read about began in conversations that arguably didn't actually go very well.

All the healing, transformation and breakthroughs on any scale began in conversations that went well. Take any event in any media, any public debate and movement for better or worse and trace them back to countless conversations that perfectly resulted in what happened.

Our world as we experience it daily reflects precisely the world that comes about as the result of the sum and synergy of our conversations. Anything better tomorrow will be better because of the conversations that make them so.

We used to think it was all about money and power, religion and politics, business and culture. These are all symptomatic of the very conversations that shape them.

If we want to see these change in any way, it will because we are together authoring new conversations about them.

If we want to inspire any dimensions of our personal and social lives, it will take conversations that make a difference. We don't have to go on dramatic campaigns to reengineer our flaws, reinvent our families or reimagine our friends.

All it takes is cultivating the art of conversations.

How does it makes sense that everything comes from conversations?

What would you say have been some of the best conversations of your life and what made them best?

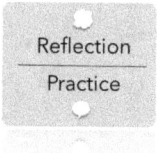

Reflection

Practice

Consider things in your life and your world that are working, not broken or going well and reflect on how conversations contribute to these.

Think about what you might consider your conversational strengths, things you often do well and enjoy, and how you could draw from those more in conversations.

# Why We Talk

It's fascinating how many reasons we have for conversation.

Intrinsically, we talk for the sheer pleasure of it. Extrinsically, we talk to make meaning possible beyond the conversation.

We are excited to share good news, gossip or tidbits. We have work to get done. We need agreement on something. We seek entertainment. We are falling short of being good company for ourselves.

We have something we want others to correct or confess. We have an ask or an offer. We have feedback. We have questions and seek someone's perspective. We want to favor someone with our perspective on their questions. We seek new, more, better connections or resources. We have a common decision to make, plan to achieve or problem to solve. We just want to express care, concern or love. We want to repair misunderstandings.

We want relief from the nags of everyday obligations. We want to feel smarter or superior to others. We want allies in our war against people who don't get, respect or love us nearly enough.

We have stories to tell, grievances to share or updates to deliver. We want to think out loud with a trusted conversational companion. We want to share a secret. We want to set a date. We want to deepen or refresh a connection.

Each of us, in each conversation opportunity, has our own reasons for conversation. Anything can spark, sustain and conclude conversations.

Of the trillions of conversations we have daily around the world, there are not trillions of conversational genres. We can categorize them into a handful of common patterns: connecting, banter, utility, tense and awkward conversations.

In connecting conversations we share personal interest in each other. We feel emotionally and mutually heard, understood and appreciated. Interest in what each other knows, feels and wants builds trust.

In banter conversations we trade updates, opinions and observations. We feel amused, entertained and informed. According to University of Surrey researcher, Nicholas Emler, 80% of our conversations are gossip, of which 90% is benign.

In utility conversations we negotiate the logistics and details of everyday business. We feel productive, aligned and resolved. We seek conclusions that answer the questions of who, when, where and which. We get decided and done what needs to be decided and done.

In tense conversations, there is a desire for some kind of closure on an emotionally charged problem, dilemma or issue. We feel uncertain, uncomfortable and irritated. Whether we want the same things, we share a tension that seeks some kind of relief or resolution.

In awkward conversations we fumble for ways to begin, continue or end a conversation. We feel tentative, unsure and unconnected. The conversation lacks interest, flow and a sense of syncing together. They are often conversations of obligation.

Banter, utility, tense and awkward conversations, however useful or welcome, do not necessarily become connecting conversations. Connecting conversations have their own unique character grounded in mutual learning about the world as seen through each other's eyes.

What kinds of conversation do you most and least look forward to and what makes them different?

How could you make any of your utility, tense and awkward conversations more emotionally connecting?

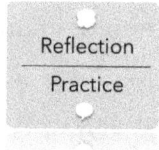

Reflection

Practice

Identify the kinds of conversations you have regularly and have coming up and consider what could make them in any ways better.

Before going into any conversation, get clear on why you're having it and make sure your why guides you along the way, being open to knowing your why could change in the conversation.

# Good Connections, Good Life

The longest study on happiness and wellbeing, now 75 years old, is the Harvard study that delivers a simple, compelling message. The highest predictor of people with the highest sustainable levels of happiness and wellbeing is the quality of their connections throughout their life.

People who instead suffer isolation do poorly on every level, including cognitive and health functioning and resilience.

As we think of conversations as the heart of connections, we realize the quality of our life is equal to the quality of our conversations. This is good news for the 94% in the global study for this book who said from a large degree to very much so it was possible to get better at conversation.

Whatever our state or status in life, we can have a deep influence over the quality of our lives simply by growing our capacity for connecting conversations.

What about your conversations make you feel a sense of positive connection to others in your life and world?

How has positive social connection made a difference in your life so far, especially in the transitions?

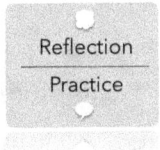

Reflection
Practice

Invite someone into conversation you don't usually have conversations with, see regularly on social media, at work or in the neighborhood, someone with whom you have things in common.

Decide how much time in an average week you would optimally give yourself for connecting conversations with people in your life and world.

# Context

Connecting conversations are valuable in an array of contexts: with strangers, new regulars, in conflicts, when reconnecting, with struggling others and in meetings.

## Strangers

The more exposure to different people we create, the more evidence we have for the vast similarities across the dizzying varieties of people on the planet. Across the 6,500 languages spoken today, we share resonating stories. It can take just minutes to realize an emotional connection with someone we don't or barely know. Everyone we consider our most intimate and significant others began as strangers, starting with our mothers. We grew into closeness one connecting conversation at a time.

The more connecting conversations we have with strangers, the more connected we feel to the world. The more at home in it we feel. The more we care about the wellbeing of over seven billion cousins in the human family.

**New regulars**

New people enter our life, often without our choosing, through our connections with others. They are neighbors and family, friends and coworkers. We mutually benefit from creating, sustaining and growing these connections each time through connecting conversations.

We want easy, satisfying connections with them, with few costs. The more connected we are, the more benefits outscale costs. We don't have to be intimately connected to them. Connections with regulars are not givens. They are co-created and co-narrated.

## Conflicts

Connecting conversations prevent and smooth conflicts with people in our lives. They grow trust. Trust is the difference between a prevented and rather smooth conflict and one that creates tension, division and unwanted costs.

Conflicts are inevitable because so many of life's questions appear as either-or and no two people know the same world in the same way. Conflicts require the both-and of creativity, which is only possible for people who enjoy some level of shared trust. In connection, we are smarter together and everyone benefits.

## Reconnecting

We lose touch, we drift apart, we lose connection. Reconnection happens through iterations of connecting conversations.

As we move into reconnection, the reasons for disconnection fade in significance. Connecting conversations bring us into the present. They refresh mutual interest in what now matters and each other. We begin to restore our shared conversational possibilities.

## Struggling others

Those we care about struggle. They long for a safe space, a space of knowing they can be heard, understood and affirmed.

Connecting conversations create this space for them. Only in being free to be vulnerable can they find their strength. Feeling connected, they no longer feel alone on their path. They can listen more deeply and see possibilities not evident in isolation.

## Meetings

In our better meetings, we get things done. Everyone contributes. Everyone feels free to contribute, co-create and commit to what matters to us together.

This is more possible when we feel a sense of emotional connection. Disconnected people get stuck together in more arguing than agreement and excuses than action. In connecting conversations, we find ways to do together what no one can do alone, in isolation or opposition.

Connecting conversations make all this possible. In each context, it is our ability and willingness to be emotionally connected that opens space for good things. Life is that much easier and richer. The quality of our efforts equal the quality of our conversations.

When can you invite more connecting conversations in your everyday and weekend routines?

What do you think your life would be like if you increased even by a small percentage the number of connecting conversations you have in any given week?

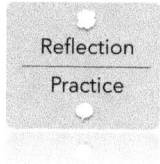

Reflection
Practice

Make a point of starting more brief conversations with strangers in common spaces, such as in any context of waiting together, as random acts of kindness.

Aim to have a connecting conversation with someone different every week.

# Connecting Conversations

The global study for this book indicates some clear patterns in how people think about connecting conversations.

91% of the 285 respondents report they experience emotionally connected conversations when they feel a sense of mutual presence, trust and discovering something new. These are twice as important as the need to like others and have many similarities with them.

Lack of mutual trust, feeling unheard or misunderstood are the leading contributors to conversations that don't feel connected. These are over twice as disconnecting as a sense of tension, distractions or talking about things that are difficult.

The highest item that participants believe they could most likely improve in conversations, at 93%, is showing interest in others. This is equaled by helping others feel heard and understood.

This study in combination with a rich array of interviews with researchers, playwrights and film makers who study and practice the craft of conversation paint an interesting picture.

As it turns out, the practice of mutual personal interest in each other shapes all the key variables in connecting conversations: presence, trust, feeling heard and understood and discovering new things.

Mutual interest distinguishes connecting conversations from banter, utility, tense and awkward conversations where these spaces are more about talking than learning. Connecting is shared listening and learning about each other.

When you think about the conversations that feel most connecting for you, what makes them so?

What do you think you personally do to contribute to connecting conversations in your life and world?

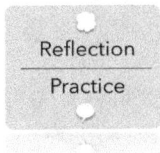

Reflection
Practice

Go into conversations with an intention for learning as much as talking.

To move any conversation from banter, utility, tense and awkward to connecting, make it more possible for others to feel heard and understood.

# Banter and Utility Conversations

Banter and utility conversations make up the lion's share of how many of us daily interact. On any given day, there can be a lot of opinions, updates, gossip and decisions to share. With our significant life and work others, there are miles of details to coordinate before we sleep. Banter and utility conversations are the social fuel that keeps harmony in our relationships humming along.

Both kinds of conversations work well when we keep them simply banter and utility without letting them slide into also becoming tense conversations. Banter and utility conversations aren't designed for tense conversational spaces.

There is a time and place for the superficial banter conversations of small talk. We simply delight in commentaries and stories. We have no agenda. We play within the lines of light and friendly. We don't have to solve or resolve anything. We don't feel urgency to draw conclusions. We enjoy common views, speculations and meanderings.

In good banter, turn taking is natural and seamless. Brief rants are welcome, as are the gifts of random insights and savoring the moments. It is just enough to float along the surface of things.

The art of superficial conversation is expression and exchange that has little or no consequence to the substance of our personal lives. These currencies include gossip, weather, news, sports, trivia, tips and entertaining anecdotes.

They can be playful and relaxing, raucous and snarky. We could easily describe some of them as fairly silly, pointless or meaningless in content.

However, they can be priceless and cherished time just to be together in the most human and genuinely affectionate ways possible.

Utility conversations work best when we remain fairly clear and flexible, otherwise it turns tense. There is no such phenomenon as over communicating in utility conversations.

Being proactive optimizes the satisfaction potential of utility conversations. There is less joy in feeling rushed and without the array of options available to the proactive.

Banter and utility conversations are most satisfying when we simply exchange what is amusing or productive. Any kind of direct or indirect personally critical remarks shift everything into bickering.

Bickering can be unilateral or shared. It usually involves small personal jabs at a vulnerability. Bickering isn't seeking a solution or resolution as much as righteous irritation sharing. Bickering's story is how much better our lives would be without the weaknesses of others and that anything good will require the successful elimination of their weaknesses.

Bickering isn't intrinsically divisive. John Gottman's work indicates that even bickering can be useful as long as it happens by agreement. As long we savor it together, bickering, even with great animation, can be a mutually amusing, benign experience.

Unilateral bickering is usually more wedge than wisdom in conversations we want to keep simply and satisfyingly banter or utility.

Unsatisfying bickering, particularly as it turns into tense arguing conversations, can signal we might benefit from shifting into connecting conversations where we let go of superficialities and problem solving to a space of emotionally connecting, mutual, personal interest. When trust is gained or restored, we can return to banter or utility with renewed simplicity or satisfaction.

What makes banter conversations most enjoyable for you and those with whom you enjoy banter?

What do you do to make utility conversations good?

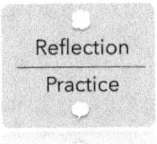

Consider ways to make bickering more from agreement and fun.

Look for ways to wedge more banter into your everyday conversational life.

# Tense and Awkward Conversations

In tense conversations, it is clear that at least one of us will not be happy until we get resolution on a problem, dilemma or issue. In a palpably more stiff than playful tone, we exchange proposals and demands, asks and offers, denials and agreements. The process of being heard and understood is at least as important as the product of resolution.

It helps to compassionately remember that each of us does the best we can at any point in time based on what we know at that time.

Banter and utility conversations can be run off the road into tense conversations by emotionally charged arguments. Differing definitions of fairness and a bias for being right over being connected add to tension.

In her TED talk, Kathryn Schulz, reminds us that it's unlikely to feel wrong when we are. At the height of our wrongness, most of us feel right. We don't feel wrong until the moment we realize it. We can be indefinitely wrong and never know it. We can both or all be wrong and have no clue we are. Millions of people can be unconsciously wrong.

Feeling right, even when we're completely wrong, is addictive because it makes us feel virtuous, successful and safe.

As we share capacity for connecting conversations, we more rarely get into tense conversations and when we do, we move through them fairly smoothly, with value added to the relationship and our individual sense of worthiness and wellbeing.

Only with the mutual trust of connecting conversations do we have the requisite creativity to craft mutually satisfying and skillful approaches to agreement. As valid as tension feels, it just doesn't have the power to reveal new possibilities the way connection does. That's why we can get stuck in tension together for any length of time.

There is little evidence that pushing our agenda results in mutually satisfying outcomes. In every case, getting beyond tense conversations takes a certain measure of collaborative creativity, growing ideas together. New and even old ideas are at risk in tense conversations. Connecting conversations make the difference.

While tense conversations can become awkward conversations, we can have awkward conversations without tension. In awkward conversations, we have to work hard for flow and sync. We feel stymied by the chasm of differences between us.

As we cultivate our capacity for connecting conversations, we lose our capacity for awkward conversations.

As we have more connecting conversations with strangers, we increasingly become suspicious that we have more in common with others than the assumed chasm of our differences might otherwise suggest.

How does it makes sense that when any of us makes a conversation tense, we're not necessarily trying to make life difficult, it's just that we're frustrated?

What would ease the transition from tense to connecting conversations?

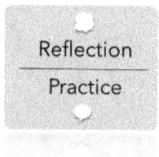

Reflection
Practice

Take the initiative to be the first in a tense conversation to express personal interest in another, with questions a friend would ask them.

Practice the five growing ideas nutrients, described later in the book, as you explore options in tense conversations.

# It Takes Two, And One

In a conversational pairing, it takes both to create connecting conversations. One can't do it. It's not enough for one person to speak, listen or inquire. It's not enough for one person to feel trusted or trusting.

One person can make a difference. One can create an infectious tone of empathy, interest, storytelling and fun. One can invite a comfortable sense of vulnerability and trust. One can be present enough to calm the energy so everyone is less reactive and distracted.

One person can keep the fluency alive with new questions, stories and transitions. One can invite a new conversation, new focus, new agreement or new participant.

This book is designed to be enjoyed alone or shared. Two or more people in regular conversation can use it to mutually grow shared capacity for connecting conversations in ways not possible by any one person's best individual efforts.

With whom could you share parts of this book to practice together?

What could you do individually to move any upcoming conversations into more connecting conversations?

Reflection

Practice

Consider any routine banter and utility conversion and improvise how to make them more connecting.

Consider any upcoming tense conversation and explore how you can start it off in a more connecting tone.

# Conversational Essentials

# Beginnings

There are as many ways to begin good conversations as there are stars and galaxies.

Conversations can begin in stories, anecdotes, questions, updates, gossip, complaints, appreciations, asks, offers, agreements, dissents, refusals, repairs and returns to previous finished and unfinished conversations. A conversation can begin sitting quietly together.

What happens after the beginning is more important to a conversation's potential goodness. A conversation beginning with "Why do you love me?" in any media can last seconds. One that begins with "Have you seen my socks?" can go on for hours, even days.

No single beginning has the intrinsic power to launch a good or bad conversation. It's all about what happens next and beyond the initial invitation.

This is particularly significant when we anticipate a tense or awkward conversation. What starts out potentially or actually tense and awkward can move quickly into a utility, banter or connecting conversation. It's all about our personal and shared ability to create transitions beyond the opening invitation.

When we get good at inviting and engaging in transitions, we can move fluently between all genres of conversations. When we aren't good at transitions, we get stuck in one or the other, usually whichever opens the conversation.

Even though we can begin any conversation anywhere, including something provocative or contentious, how we begin sets a tone that can unreasonably shape the contours of the path ahead.

How many different ways do you have for beginning conversations with anyone in your life and world?

What would be new ways to begin conversations?

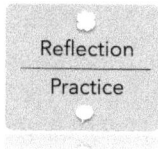

Reflection
Practice

Going into conversations, be intentional about the emotional tone you want to set.

Start more conversations with new and open questions.

# Endings

Every conversation has its own unique ending.

Some conversations end abruptly, unintentionally. We exit together because some unplanned event takes us away. Some just wind down and dissolve as we move onto other conversations or something else. Some are ended implicitly.

Sometimes we know each other well enough to know that a certain tone or tempo transition signals a conclusion. Sometimes we end intentionally and explicitly. We announce some kind of appreciation, acknowledgement, conclusions, anticipation of our next conversation or a combination of these.

When we explicitly clarify how much time we each comfortably have for a conversation, we make it possible to time things so the conversation doesn't end just as we're in the thick of things important, sensitive, unfinished or enjoyable.

When we want an exit or break, we can make it more comfortable by making our excuse clear, sincere and meaningful. An exit after some form of acknowledgment, conclusion or appreciation is much more comfortable than anything abrupt or worse. Worse includes ending with parting insults, attacks or still going on about ourselves.

When an exit is an obvious movement to another conversation, we can simply and sincerely share our motivation for the next conversation, as in "I've been meaning to talk to ... about ..."

The most satisfying endings end in some kinds of expression of connection.

What makes for good endings to connecting conversations?

What signals do you give people that a conversation is winding down for you?

Make a point in any extended or important conversations to find out about how much time people have so endings aren't unnecessarily surprising or abrupt.

End every conversation with something positive like a statement of appreciation or wish.

## Turn Taking

In connecting conversations, no one dominates. Whether in conversations of two, three or more, no one does most of the talking. No one goes on and on pontificating, ranting, lecturing or taking all the attention, no matter how compelling, entertaining or important their story, report or message.

No one becomes a black hole sucking the life out of the fluency of the space, leaving others disengaged bystanders.

People take turns. Optimally two things happen. We pay attention to signals of turn taking. We notice leaning in, faces poised to speak and gestures of readiness. We offer signals. We don't make others guess when we're ready to take turns.

This is all easier in a visual conversation, in person or video call, and possibly more tricky in a phone call and text. It helps in text when we use a smart app that allows us to see others typing in real time.

We can give cues in the rhythm and tone of our cadence, slowing down and shifting our tone in ways that invites the next turn. Questions are the most obvious and explicit ways to invite turn taking.

Conversational quality is richer when the rhythm is even between and among everyone in the conversation. The more shared the rhythm, the better the conversation feels.

Brevity is key to turn taking. The more briefly we talk, relative to the overall length and tempo of the conversation, the more chances we have for better rhythm and flow.

We do conversations a favor anytime we insert ourselves into the flow of someone who is dominating. We have to do this, uncomfortable as it might feel, for the sake of the quality of the rhythm and flow.

We have to do this even when the dominator holds actual or perceived higher status or emotional neediness, as in the case of talking to a boss, parent, expert, or someone who feels the need to be in control.

Fluency is flow. Flow has rhythm and speed. Each conversation has its own unique rhythm between talking and pausing, back and forth. The flow has rhythm. Each conversational genre tends to have its own rhythm.

Banter has faster flow, sometimes more staccato, than connecting conversations. Tense and awkward conversations have more jagged and uneven flow. Utility conversations can vary in speed and rhythm.

Fluency is most possible in text if each turn follows immediately, more synchronously than asynchronously. Otherwise, the unpredictable rhythms and speeds can keep conversations more suited to banter and utility conversations. It's more tricky to move from tense and awkward to banter or connecting conversations in text because of flow issues.

Even moving to phone when visual isn't available can restore the flow necessary for the transition from banter, utility and tense to connecting conversations.

What is the relationship between turn taking and the quality of conversation?

What are the costs of dominating or allowing anyone to dominate any conversation, formal or informal?

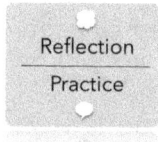

Reflection
Practice

When someone dominates a conversation, for any reason, look for a natural inhale or pause and initiate a question or response.

Make your turns short enough for people to take turns at a lively tempo.

# Transitions

Conversations flow well because of transitions.

Transitions can be questions, interesting tidbits that pique curiosity, invitations to new topics, twists and turns, reactions that spark counter-reactions and resonant stories evoking others. They naturally lead us to the next thing in the conversation.

It's possible to become more intentional about inserting transitions in conversations that would otherwise become awkward or tense. Transitions move conversations along a path usually more co-improvised than planned.

It's good practice to give ourselves the luxury of listening to good conversations to study how people naturally use transitions to sustain and grow conversational fluency. It's an art form as high as any art form. The variety of transitions are only limited to our capacity for creative imagination and improvisation.

The more we get to know people, the more possible it is to invite a transition that has personal interest and relevance to them. With a simple engaging reference to something we know about them like "You know, you've …" we invite them to take the conversation into a next or new direction.

Making it more possible for others to invite transitions is giving cue rich responses to questions. This means instead of reacting with single words to a question asking for single word answers, we respond with details, stories, anecdotes, context or insights into our experience.

We can add why and how we did something, not just what. When we ask questions, we can ask for how and why rather than just what, when or who.

Single word responses also make it more likely others won't be able to have new stepping stones to new conversational streams. Cue-rich responses give them more transition possibilities.

We cultivate our capacity for transitions when we rely more on our own intuition and imagination than on something from our phones. We're seeing whole conversations where people just take turns showing each other things on their phones.

There is no limit to the possibilities of inserting transitional references and questions into any parts of any conversations. It's cultivating a sensibility about giving others something new to respond to, interact with and inspire the conversational flow.

What causes conversational flow?

Why can some conversations lose steam after a few minutes and others go on for hours?

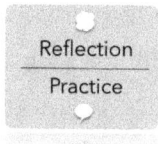

Reflection

Practice

Listen for transition cues from others in conversations to take the flow into new and different directions.

Use rich responses to others that have enough content for a variety of transitions options.

# Pauses

Pauses amplify the emotions at play. When a conversation feels awkward or tense, pauses amplify these. When a conversation feels tender, caring and connecting, pauses amplify these as well. This applies to pauses within and during turn taking.

In conversations of greater trust, more and longer pauses feel welcome. In conversations where trust is unknown or low, pauses are better fewer and more brief. Gradually inserting and lengthening pauses can make them more welcome.

A global study of languages indicate that across cultures, better conversations feature minimal pauses between conversational turns.

In connecting conversations, pauses create a deeper, more reflective experience. Not introducing or allowing pauses keeps conversations at more superficial and less connecting levels. People who fill every potential pause with talking or asking prevent even the kind of connection they seek or could otherwise enjoy.

We feel more present to others when we allow and insert pauses in conversations.

Are there ways and times you naturally pause in conversations?

Where in connecting conversations could you invite pauses that add value?

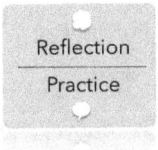

Reflection
Practice

In an upcoming conversation you want to be more connecting, insert more pauses, keeping their duration comfortable in the natural rhythm of the conversation.

Resist filling silences too quickly in conversations where insights or emotions are deeper.

## Tell Me More

95% of people participating in the study for this book believe that trust is vital to connecting conversations.

Three words can easily and quickly spark conversational trust: "Tell me more." They can be explicitly stated or conveyed in our tone of voice, posture or gestures. They communicate an open space of acceptance, invitation and hospitality. We feel acknowledged and affirmed. We trust each other and the conversation.

Trust makes honesty, humility and genuineness possible. We feel more free to talk and ask without edit. We share more personally. We feel more free to propose and accept agreements on what matters about how we interact with each other. We learn more about what each other knows, feels, thinks and wants. It becomes more possible for conversations to make a difference.

What do you believe mutual trust makes possible in conversations?

What does mistrust and suspicion make possible?

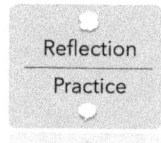

Reflection
Practice

Make a habit of inserting into more conversations "Tell me more…" in variations, even when others come across as if they have already told us all they know.

Especially when others are emotionally charged about something, give them the gift of uninterrupted space to speak, without any attempt to try to interrupt with solutions or advice.

# Kind Inquiry

It's wise to judge our questions by their results rather than our intentions. What we pre-assess as a potentially great, terrible, honest or weak question could end up being received as the opposite. It has to do with texture and timing.

Texture is the emotional charge of the language. One word can change the result of a question. Why is harsher than how. How is a gentler question that creates more space for people to feel comfortable being honest. Either-or questions are harsher than both-and questions. Should is harsher than could and would. Which is harsher than when.

Instead of bullying others into a decision, we ask them to instead consider the gentler question of under what kinds of conditions they would choose one path or another. Any judgmental word in a question signals that honest dialogue in mutual learning is unwelcome, intolerable or grounds for negative judgment.

Conversations decline in quality to the degree that people feel cornered rather than valued by our questions. Harsh questions come across as having right and wrong answers, with the subtle or explicit implication that we confer on ourselves the power to be the ultimate arbiters of right and wrong.

Timing is everything. Even though many of our best questions will be new questions that others could feel unprepared for, they are questions people might feel ready to ponder, explore and reflect on with us.

The problem with old questions is they result in old stories, old opinions and old conclusions. People are too ready for them. Their best timing was days, weeks, months or years ago. They invite the disengagement of monologues.

Good questions have currency of relevance. They are relevant to what's most interesting, urgent or important to the present. Even when we ask new questions about the distant past or future, they feel entirely relevant to our experience in the present.

Information questions ask for information only. Connecting questions don't just ask for information, they ask for insights into the way others think, feel, decide that have the potential to lead to stories or anecdotes.

Instead of "Did you see...?" we could ask "Do you have a favorite news source?" Instead of "Where do you like to go out to eat?" we could ask "How do you decide on new restaurants?" Instead of "Have you ever been to...?" we could ask "Would you spend a month anywhere and why?" Instead of "How long have you lived in ...? we could ask "What do you want your next house to be like?"

Instead of "What do you do?" we could ask "How has your week been?" Instead of "What do you think about ... (any news, weather, sports topics)?" we could ask "What would surprise you about ...?" Instead of "Have you seen, heard from, talked to ...?" we could ask "What do you most appreciate about ...?"

What are ways you could use new questions in conversations to create new conversations with people?

What makes questions feel like caring questions to others?

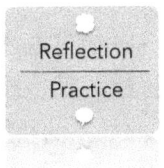

Reflection

Practice

When anticipating a conversation, think about what kinds of connecting instead of informational questions you can ask.

When crafting new questions, consider varying questions by varying forms including who, what, when, where, how, why, which, what if.

# Reports and stories

A report is a linear account of events, facts and opinions. We dispense gossip, travelogues and commentaries on anything. People listen for things they can use to volley back their own reporting.

Stories feel distinctly different. As soon as a story begins, our interest is engaged. Something catches our curiosity. We look forward to hearing more. We want to hear how it turns out because we are engaged in some kinds of questions from the start.

As reports start and end with lists of conversational things, stories begin with raising a question in another's mind that the ending answers. Stories have distinctly different structures than reports.

We can turn any report into a story simply by evoking curiosity early on and concluding it with satisfying that curiosity.

"So we got to the hotel and unpacked. Then we went to find a restaurant..." Everyone knows this is a report not a story. "I never imagined yesterday would end as it did. It started out..." Everyone feels a story, not a report, coming on.

Princeton research tells us the kind of abstract language often used in reports have no impact on the emotional centers in the brain. Storytelling uses sensory and emotional language that impacts the parts of the brain related to understanding, empathy and generosity.

Researchers at the University of Pennsylvania find that donors will give twice as much to stories as facts and figures. Stories activate emotional brain chemicals that make it feel real in ways facts do not. Facts activate the judging not generosity parts of the brain.

Cognitive psychologist Jerome Bruner tell us stories are 22 times more powerful than just report style facts in creating trust and empathy. We don't volunteer and donate to causes. We volunteer and donate to stories.

It's useful to shape stories for the tempo of the conversation. When the conversation is brief, we create brief versions of even the longest stories.

When we have more time, we create longer versions to fit the tempo of the conversation by weaving multiple shorter stories together that share similar themes, messages, characters or contexts.

Conversations are most connecting when they engage the curiosity of others. When we share stories, we can interject questions relevant to others within and throughout any story so they are participants rather than audience.

These questions ask if they have had similar experiences or stories. If other stories emerge and we have time, we go back to continue and finish stories in progress. What's important is stories don't become monologues that prevent the kind of turn taking that makes for connecting conversations.

When others turn their stories into monologues, we can interject insertions and overlaps to enliven the conversation without creating interruptions to their flow.

How do stories impact how you feel in contrast to reports?

When would stories amplify your ability to connect with, influence and amuse others in your life and world?

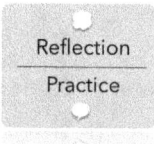

Reflection
Practice

Build your portfolio of possible stories to share in any regularly anticipated conversational opportunities.

Take time to craft stories in ways that spark and satisfy the curiosity of others.

# Repair

In the possible pitfalls of too much or too little self-editing, we are not accurately understood.

We say what we didn't exactly mean. Others get the wrong impression. We leave out enough information that makes it easy for others to harbor inaccurate assumptions. What we say or ask is not taken as intended.

We knowingly or unknowingly present contradictions that make sense to us but evoke unacceptable confusion or misunderstanding for others. Our talking gets ahead of our thinking. We seek repair.

In conversational repair, we correct or clarify what has become misunderstood, a source of tension or an opportunity for feeling better heard.

We segue into "What I meant to say ..." and "What I mean is ..." We invite others to repair as well, asking them questions from which they can correct and clarify. Inviting repair is the conversational opposite to criticism, judgment and assumption.

Repair requires intuitive attention to how others react and respond to us. Signals for repair include a withdrawal into non-responsiveness, a launch into being offended or a deflection into the most superficial banter possible.

The signals can be subtle or overt. The most skillful in disguise can effectively conceal their reactions and responses so even the most sensitive and empathetic among us would not easily know it's time for conversational repair.

A simple "Did you mean …?" can invite repair by others. It gives them a soft landing from a hard place.

What from others could signal a good opportunity for us to do some conversational repair?

What kinds of inaccurate assumptions could people have about us from our conversations?

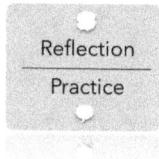

Reflection
Practice

In any kind of conversation, listen for clues that there might not be a match between what we intend others to hear from us and what it appears they are hearing.

In doing any kind of conversational repair, take rather than give responsibility for any kind of necessary clarifications.

# Insertions, Overlaps and Interruptions

Insertions are simple, brief additions, acknowledgements and affirmations. They don't interrupt someone's flow. They are things like "Yes…," "Absolutely…" and "I saw that…" Overlaps are the same only talking at the same time someone else as they continue uninterrupted.

It's unclear whether others are accustomed to insertions and overlaps unless we know from experience they are or we try a few out to see if they work.

A worldwide study of 10 major world languages shows that there is a general avoidance of overlapping in conversations. So a general rule is to not make a habit of overlapping.

Both can energize the flow and aliveness of the conversation. Notice how the most animated conversations feature generous portions of insertions and overlaps.

If they aren't brief and simple enough, they can become interruptions. Others stop talking to give us the floor.

Each of us has our own relationship to giving and receiving interruptions. To learn another's interruption biases, we can observe them with others and experiment with them. Most easily, we talk about it. We talk about when interruptions from and to them are welcome, tolerated and intolerable for them and us.

When are you most and least likely to interrupt others, and in both cases, why?

Do you use any kind of positive insertions in your conversations now?

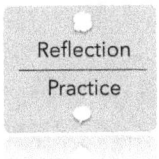

Reflection
Practice

Make a point to gracefully interrupt anyone dominating a conversation.

Practice allowing a two beat pause when it looks like someone is finished with a thought or question before taking your turn next.

## Feedback and Advice

Part of being present in conversation is being attentive to another's interest in feedback and advice. Sometimes they want it, other times they don't.

The only way to know for sure is directly ask. We can accommodate their ambivalence of no with postponing it or asking if they might want it at another time. We can accommodate their yes with asking what they might find most useful instead of assuming we know.

Most of us are more receptive to feedback and advice we opt into rather than what is imposed on us, even with the kindest or best intentions. "Would some feedback or advice be helpful right now?" gives us choice. Having choice opens us up. Not having choice shuts us down to even the best feedback and advice money can't buy.

Postponed feedback and advice erode trust. For many of us, it is intolerable to discover feedback and advice we could have benefited from when it could have initially been available.

This is why annual performance reviews are intrinsically loathed and toxic. A Society for Human Resources Management survey reports that 2% of US managers give their people ongoing feedback.

We can repair poorly timed feedback and advice by backing up into more understanding of their context and experience. The more we know what they know, the more useful our contributions and offerings become.

Humility goes further than arrogance or thinly veiled or overt criticism. Positive feedback preceding negative is more easily digestible.

Perhaps the most connecting feedback is gratitude. Research from UC, Berkeley finds that couples practicing gratitude demonstrate more commitment and responsiveness with each other than any other expression.

Who in your life and world do you give and withhold regular feedback, and why?

How do you feel when you give people positive, appreciative or grateful feedback?

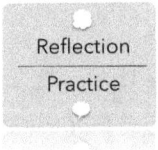

Reflection

Practice

Before offering advice or feedback, ask people if, when, how and why they might want it.

Find ways to give people more grateful than critical feedback.

# Humor

Humor can be a rich nutrient in connecting conversations. It depends on the kinds of humor used and everyone's capacity for enjoying humor. Humor can connect or disconnect.

Connecting humor is the celebration of life's paradoxes, ironies and inconsistencies. Everything funny reveals some kind of incongruity, something other than expected, as in the punch line.

Humor comes in many forms from self-deprecating humor, jokes, puns, pranks, sarcasm, irreverence, kidding, teasing, exaggeration, understatement, stories, mimicry and situational lightheartedness.

Positive humor lightens conversational energy. Many of us trust people with a sense of humor we enjoy more than with those without. It is no coincidence there is a shared linguistic root among humanity, humility and humor.

In what kinds of conversations would some humor add positive energy?

What kinds of positive humor did you used to have that might be valuable reviving, even in a different form?

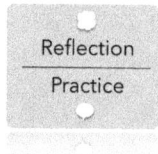

Reflection
Practice

In any upcoming conversation, look for ways to inject even a bit of mild humor.

Spend time working on identifying and crafting your stories that feature some kind of humor or amusement.

## Contagious Energy

Emotional energy is contagious, especially when we're in physical proximity to others, as in within a few feet or meters. Our heart energy directly impacts one another in this space.

It matters what we talk about. We emit, evoke and escalate positive energy every time we talk about what we do want, do have and can do. We create the same negative contagious energy every time we talk about what we don't want, don't have and can't do.

It takes nothing but simple language shifts to translate negatives into positives and create a completely different heart vibration.

Visuals count. A single physical or virtual smile can make a world of difference between caution and comfort. Fortunately, smiles register the same kinds of joy and warmth across cultures. Few smiles are wasted in connecting conversations.

Researcher Christine Porath finds that with just a smile and simple thank you people are perceived as 27% warmer and 13% more competent.

University of Chicago and Harvard researchers found that negotiators who shook hands were more open and honest and reached better outcomes. Shaking hands causes the centers of the brain associated with rewards to activate.

Albert Mehrabian, a major contributor in the study of non-verbal communication suggests the degree of liking conveyed by facial expressions dominate and determine the impact of the total message.

Italian neuroscientist Giacomo Rizzolatti and colleagues developed the idea of mirror neurons. When you see a person take some action, your brain fires up the neurons associated with the same action. When your conversation partner smiles, a part of your brain smiles too. Your smile resonates in their brain as well.

What do you do to express contagious positive energy in conversations?

When would contagious positive energy best add value to your conversations?

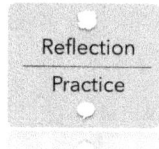

Reflection

Practice

Notice when new people enter conversations and how their emotional energy affects the energy already there.

Anytime you notice you're talking about what you don't want, don't have and can't do quickly shift to what you do want, do have and can do.

# Connecting Conversations

## Emotional Connection

When we feel emotionally connected with another, we feel a sense of home. We feel invited and welcome to be interested in what each other knows, feels and wants. We feel interested and interesting, cared about and caring, trusted and trusting.

There are no limits. While we sustain a small circle of significants and friends, we feel emotionally connected to any number of people from those we've known forever to those we will encounter only once and others we've just recently met. Mutual interest reveals the bonds of our likenesses.

Stanford research indicates that people who feel the belonging of similarities automatically sync with the motivations of those they share with. People's heart rates beat in sync with an emotionally bonded partner simply by being next to their partner jogging in place. Connected people endure longer, experience flow more and get more done.

Brigham Young University researchers Lori Schade and Jonathan Sandberg find that being constantly connected through technology can create disconnects in committed relationships. Using text messages to apologize, work out differences or make decisions is associated with lower relationship quality for women.

Too frequent texting is associated with lower relationship quality for men. In contrast, for women and men, expressing affection via text enhances the relationship.

MIT researcher Sherry Turkle talks about how visual conversations unfold slowly. They teach and require the kind of patience more uncommon in text conversations. They cultivate the kind of self-reflection that enriches connections with ourselves and others. This is true of visual in person as well as tech media like video calls.

Not surprisingly, other studies indicate that our emotional connections tend to be strongest in visual, then phone and finally text conversations.

Who are the people in your life and world with whom it's important to feel an emotional connection, and why?

What benefits do phone and visual conversations offer over text in an intention for emotional connection?

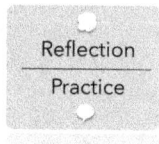

Consider ways to shift some text conversations to phone and visual conversations.

Think about whom you might like to feel more emotionally connected to and invite connecting conversations in the next week.

# Connection Worthiness

One of the classic definitions of worthiness is capacity. Seaworthy vessels had the capacity to fare on the seas.

Each of us comes to conversations with our own sense of connection worthiness, our capacity for connection. Some of us delight in connecting conversations. The more, more variety and deeper the better. Our capacity is wide and deep.

Others of us, not so much. We are somewhere between hesitant and resistant to emotionally connecting conversations.

They by definition cannot be predictable spaces and are wrought with levels of uncertainty we don't have capacity for.

With a long standing love for predictability and control, we prefer the more shallow waters of banter and utility conversations. Connecting conversations involve the kind of vulnerability and trust that eludes a sense of predictability and control.

Connecting conversations create a sense of emotional closeness. For some of us it becomes an emotional intimacy.

For a variety of reasons, some us simply don't have the emotional receptors to process emotional intimacy. We honestly feel overwhelmed, fear, unworthiness. We don't have capacity to process all the feelings and uncertainties that are intrinsic to connecting conversations.

While we have capacity to engage in friendliness and even physical closeness and sexual intimacy, we keep emotional intimacy at a safe distance.

The good news is that the more people are invited into potentially connecting conversations, the more they learn to trust the space. The more we invite others who love connecting conversation into them, the more we can grow our own capacity for them. The richer our lives become.

What would tell us that someone is not comfortable with emotionally connecting conversations?

How would we communicate to others that we are comfortable with emotionally connecting conversations?

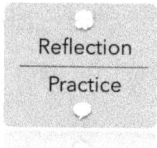

Reflection
Practice

In relationships of mostly banter, utility, tense and awkward conversations, improvise with new ways to spend short amount of time in more connecting conversation.

With people who seem less prone to emotionally connecting conversations, practice doing things to create a more comfortable space with them.

## Showing Interest

In connecting conversations, we show personal interest in others. They feel our interest in what they know, feel and want. This is interest in what they say and ask, and beyond to what they aren't.

Even when we're just trading information or transacting agreements, our personal interest in their perspective, their experience, their view is clear and palpable to them.

This is the kind of personal interest where knowing more about each other is the intention, not just knowing more about other people and things.

Showing interest in others is the opposite of talking about what only interests us. Two or more people volleying back and forth makes for good banter or utility conversations. The conversation becomes emotionally connecting when mutual interest in each other's inner experience inspires, animates and informs the conversation.

When people feel our interest in them, they have a palpable sense that we're always more interested in discovering more about them than simply focusing in what they're talking about.

Tracking anyone's social media posts can give us instant entrees into being interested in them. "I saw you ..." is a simple, comfortable way to initiate interest in any conversation. We take time in preparation for conversations by scanning through someone's recent posts to discover interest opportunities.

Many others likely assume we're interested when we stay silent as they speak. They only know the reality and quality of our interest by our questions.

The likelihood that others feel heard and understood comes about because of the quality of our interest, expressed through the quality of our questions.

Listening has an unreasonably strong impact on our ability to inspire and influence others. A study of leaders and employees of a large hospital system found that listening explained 40% of the variance in the quality and effectiveness of leadership.

At its core, interest is a humble sense of awe, the realization that there is a universe to be discovered beyond the footprint of the known, that there is so much we don't know. At the heart of interest is knowing that and what we don't know.

University of California, Irvine studies show that the experience of awe reduces narcissism and materialism and increases a sense of connection, generosity and courage. They describe awe as feeling part of something larger than oneself, like the universe awaiting discovery in every connecting conversation.

Stanford research indicates that awe, more than happiness, causes us to feel like we have an abundance of time to generously share with others. This is good news when we feel short on time to give to others who matter most to us.

Interest in others causes them to feel more connected in and trusting of us. At the same time, it transforms who we are.

Why is showing genuine, personal, mutual interest in each other more rare in conversations, especially banter, tense and awkward conversations?

Why do we feel naturally more trusting of people who share mutual interest with us?

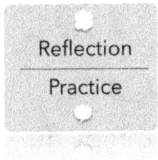

Reflection
Practice

In a connecting conversation, instead of just talking, ask questions to learn more about how others think and feel.

In conversations, listen for context not just content; show kind interest in *why* people think and feel as they do.

# Being Interesting

Two things make us interesting in conversations, interest and relevance.

We become interesting in our interest in others. Others naturally find us as interesting as we show interest in them.

When we talk about things that are relevant to others, we become more interesting to them. They feel more connected to us. Relevance has two dimensions. We talk about what they are already familiar with and the edge of their questions.

Relevance is relative. With all the assuming we can do, even with people we believe we know well, we cannot know what another is interested in talking about at any given point in time until we actually find out. Others can be more interested in things they're not talking about than in those they are. We stay curious rather than assumptive about the live interests of others.

When we know people's current and persistent interests, the probabilities of our being relevant to those are positive. The more relevant we are to others, the more interesting we are and the more interesting and connecting the conversation becomes.

This becomes most possible when we stay open to the possibility that even our most daily and familiar others have interests emerging unexpressed and outside our knowing until our curiosity invites them into conversation.

How might being interesting to others benefit you and them?

What would your conversations be like if you became more interesting?

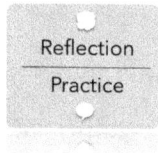

Get to know the interests of others more so you can make your conversations with them more relevant to their interests.

Practice more curiosity with people you think you know best, especially finding out what else interests them currently beyond what they talk about.

# The Art of Growing Interest

Some people can go on for hours of conversation and never ask a single personal question to others in the conversation. They can be very engaged and not explicitly express personal interest. This can happen between spouse and partners, friends and family, acquaintances and coworkers.

We create connecting conversations when we help others get more interested in us and others.

Not everyone is accustomed to showing interest in conversations. It's not a habit. Their personal struggles absorb all their attention capacities. They only listen to speak more. They have never developed the inquiry portfolio and agility to think of new, engaging questions on the spot. They were taught good fences make good neighbors.

They expect that as long as everyone keeps talking about whatever they want to talk about, others will equally reciprocate, making intentional questions unnecessary.

"Did you know ...?" is a simple way to invite curiosity in others. It opens a space of curiosity for them. It primes their curiosity pump. It gives permission for wonder, for questions and awe.

It's particularly useful when we have been asking all the questions with few or none reciprocated from others to us. "Do you ever wonder...?" is an effective way to elicit and invite their curiosity.

A more subtle approach is to use interest rich language. Every word and phrase we use has different potential to attract the interest of others. When asked about our day, we can use interest weak language like "same old, same old" or "pretty busy." Interest rich language about the same day could include references to "best/worst meeting of the week."

Interest rich language is a brief reference implying there is more to the story, or even new stories altogether. They create an immediate sense of potentially interesting ambiguity or paradox. They make it more possible to raise expressed questions in the minds and imaginations of others. They are the language of good storytelling.

It's possible to produce volumes of interest weak language. There are words and phrases that don't evoke curiosity. It feels like there is nothing else beyond what has already been conveyed. We create more connecting conversations when we do anything to invite others into more animated spaces of curiosity and interest.

Are there any ways we might unintentionally make ourselves not or less interesting to others?

What about ourselves do we want others to be interested in?

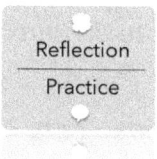

Reflection
Practice

For others who talk primarily about themselves and what they think, consider some interest rich language.

Think about questions that could get others being curious in what we and others are talking about.

# Beautiful Questions

John M. Gottman, executive director of the Relationship Research Institute, has been studying marriage and divorce for the past 35 years. He was once asked what one piece of advice he would give for a happy marriage. He suggested asking about each other's dreams.

From a collaboration last year with positive psychology partner Jen Margolis, here are 36 connecting questions, scientifically designed to create richer connections in each section.

They are inspired by a study by the psychologist Arthur Aron that explores whether intimacy between two strangers can be accelerated by having them ask each other an increasingly connecting series of personal questions. They have the power to launch new connecting conversations, even with people familiar to us, people with whom we have had years of conversations.

**1**

1. If you lived your life in another country which would you like and why?
2. What are your favorite ways to get unplugged and refreshed?
3. What kinds of friends were you drawn to growing up?
4. Did you have any favorite parents, grandparents, aunts or uncles?
5. If you could choose any actor to play you in your life story, who would it be?
6. What do you feel grateful for?
7. Do you have any morning or evening rituals?
8. Do you have preferred modes of communication, when and why?

9. What's a smell, taste and texture that makes you happy?
10. What personal accomplishments are you proud of?
11. What would you consider the qualities of a best friend?
12. What would you say you are passionate about?

**2**

1. What qualities in your friends would you tolerate for the sake of the friendship?
2. What about yourself are you currently working on?
3. What would you say are three things that are and are not true about you?
4. If you could eliminate any oppression in the world, what would you choose?

5. What is an example of a big lesson you took from growing up?

6. What would you say are differences you appreciate in others?

7. What are things you tend to be good at putting off?

8. What kinds of first impressions do you think you give others?

9. What kinds of things would you include in a perfect day?

10. What do you and your partner have in common?

11. If you could acquire a super power, what might it be?

12. If you had the attention of everyone in the world for one minute, what would you say?

**3**

1.  Which of your friends would like your partner and why?
2.  What are two things you'd like to know more about your partner?
3.  If you could have any one you know with you in your last days, who would it be?
4.  If you were reincarnated into the next life, which gender would you prefer being?
5.  What about your life right now feels like you're at a crossroads?
6.  If you could give your partner a gift right now, what would it be?
7.  What place does vulnerability have for you in close relationships?
8.  What could someone do that would make them attractive to you?
9.  What are three things you like about your partner?

10. What for you are examples of difficult feedback to give others?
11. To what age do you want to live and why?
12. What would you do this year if you knew you would live 200 years?

The simple power of these questions is in how they invite new reflections, stories and insights we might not have articulated or explored before. Each level deepens the dialogue. Each question is personal, inviting exploration of what we know, feel and want beyond what we might already know about each other.

They are beautiful questions, questions that create the space for us to fall into connection together.

What kinds of questions could someone ask you that would make you feel very cared about?

What kinds of questions have you not asked people you know well, maybe that you once asked but haven't asked for awhile?

Reflection

Practice

Plan time with anyone you'd like to grow more of a connection and go through the first set of questions, at least.

Create and improvise your own variations on interesting questions to invite new insights into others and stories from them.

## Being Comfortable

Being comfortable for others makes it easier for them to engage in connecting conversations and to smoothly transition from banter, utility, tense and awkward to more connecting conversations.

It starts with creating an emotionally safe space. This includes genuine and relevant smiles, open gestures, sharing compliments, leaning in, keeping the turn taking tempo even, using their language, talking at their pace, talking about anything in common, easy eye contact.

Warm emotional tones can mean a friendly voice or friendly text emoticons, injecting any light humor and validating the personal truth of what they know.

In tense and awkward conversations, we can share generous doses of validation. In validation, we make it clear to others that what they're saying makes sense to us as what is true for them.

It means minimizing any kind of dominating, making everything about us, drilling people with questions, using sarcasm and unfamiliar language or references and allowing too many or long pauses.

It means being present, giving attention to any signs of distance or discomfort and transitioning into something different that could create a more comfortable space. When we're doing things naturally or intentionally to help create a comfortable space, we can take personally another's openness, candidness and transparency.

When others make you feel comfortable, what exactly do they do that creates that space for you?

What does making others feel comfortable make more possible in the conversation?

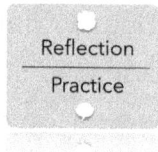

Reflection
Practice

Make it more possible for others to feel that you value whatever they talk about.

Allow yourself to physically relax throughout conversations.

# Living in a common world

Many of us share a curious mythology about the notion of an objective reality. This narrative proposes that we all live in a single, common world.

If this myth was completely accurate, we would find ourselves on a planet of complete agreement. We would all see the same one true reality without variations.

The same weather and economy would be the exactly the same for everyone. The same relationship between two people would be exactly the same for both of them. Conflict would be impossible. We would flourish in a bliss of endless consensus.

We do at times, with some people, experience a common world. When we experience a common world, it's because we come to know the same things. We take time in conversations to learn what each of us knows. The more we know together, the more we live in a common world. The common world we together get is the common world we together create.

In connecting conversations, we share more of what each of us knows. We know more together. We live in a more common world. Learning is curiosity. We inquire about what each other knows the other doesn't.

In the world before screens, people could go days, weeks and years knowing roughly the same things. They could easily live in a common world. In this screened world, we can know all kinds of things even our closest others don't. They can know all kinds of things we don't.

Competing for the single right view of the world is not a condition for enjoying a common world. Win-lose does not spark or grow connections. It sparks and grows distance and division.

Amassing hundreds of studies, researcher Alfie Kohn concludes that competition in any form, even subtle, decreases our learning potential and quality of relationships. It takes no amount of agreement to be kind with one another. Kindness takes as long as unkindness.

Our capacity for living in a common world is equal to our capacity for conversational curiosity and generosity. Sometimes just one good question or revelation can create shared knowing. Sometimes it takes layers of shared inquiry and informing.

Shared inquiry is the opposite of denying the validity of what someone knows, based on how it is something we don't know.

When we have a common world, it's because we have co-created it, not because one of us has imposed it. Inflicting our world on others is usually the least likely way toward co-creating a common world.

Researcher Charles Lord indicates that not only does more data not change people's mind, additional factual data causes them to more strongly stay attached and defensive about their beliefs.

At the heart of the most inconsolable conflicts, we lack a common world. We don't know the same things. Each point of division is about how we know different things than others. What they know as true, we don't. What we know as true, they don't.

The only way to a common world is through connection. We can't learn, understand or appreciate what someone knows that we don't until we experience the mutual trust of connecting conversations.

Until we move from tense to connecting conversations, we sustain the irreconcilability of the conflict with criticizing each other for being wrong, and worse, some unsavory combination of uncaring, ignorant, evil or disloyal.

The question possibilities are endless moving from tense to connecting conversations. Is there anything you know that you think I don't? Is there anything it would help for you to know about from me? What do we know so far that we both know?

These have the power to co-create a common world. Moving from tension to the mutual interest of connecting conversations allows us to face and transcend the fear implicit in conflicts that threaten the wellbeing of our most valued relationships.

Neuroscience research from the Weizmann Institute of Science in Rehovot indicates that exposing ourselves to what we fear energizes the courage center in our brain, that releases courage chemicals that support our acting with courage. Acting with courage stimulates feelings of courage that lead to further acts of courage.

Courage is not being without fear, it is acting contrary to our fear. Acting contrary to fear doesn't stimulate fear chemicals but courage chemicals. Connecting conversations are conversations that grow courage.

When do you feel it's ok not to be right in conversations?

With whom would you like to have a more common world together and why?

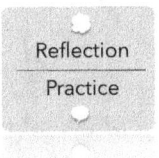

Reflection
Practice

Make curiosity your first response to disagreement in utility and tense conversations.

In an upcoming tense conversation, consider what kinds of questions you could ask to know more about what they know that you don't.

## Integrity

Integrity is transparency. We make clear what we know, feel and want. Others don't have to intuit, guess or assume rightly or wrongly what we're about and up to.

Transparency grows and sustains trustworthiness. It gives others points of intersection, of connection in interest and celebrating similarities. People can care more about us when they know us. Transparency makes this possible.

Being transparent makes it easier for others to interact with us as we actually are rather than as our personas, their assumptions about us. We put the conversational wellbeing of others at risk when we conceal and carry expectations.

There is no direct relationship between the volume and duration of our talk and the quality of our transparency. There are people who can go on and on, even loudly, and still leave us not exactly being clear what it is they specifically know, feel or want. They can be hilarious and entertaining in fairly strong non-transparency.

Our transparency makes the same more possible for others. Our transparency opens the space of possibility of mutual trustworthiness and trust.

How do you tend to make yourself transparent to others in conversations?

How could you become even more transparent to others in conversations?

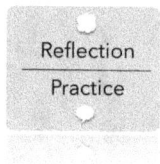

When you have wishes in a conversation for that conversation, find ways to describe them so others don't have to guess what matters to you.

Ask others what matters to them in especially connecting, utility and tense conversations.

## Intimacy

In emotional intimacy we open ourselves to interest in each other. We neither build nor maintain interest walls. We invite and engage in the kindness of tender inquiry.

Emotional intimacy isn't necessarily a given in sexual intimacy. Sexual intimacy isn't necessarily a given in emotional intimacy. Nor does the utility of sharing budgets, households or children guarantee emotional intimacy. All manner of sexual union is possible without connecting conversations.

We are as emotionally intimate as we engage together in connecting conversations.

In any kind of intimacy, touch has significant potential to create, grow and sustain a sense of emotional connection in conversation. Touching merges emotional energy fields and we feel the symbiosis of connection.

Neuroscientist Edmund Rolls reports that touch activates the brain's orbitofrontal cortex, which is linked to feelings of reward and compassion.

Touch signals safety and trust. It calms cardiovascular stress. It activates the body's vagus nerve involved in compassion and a simple touch can trigger release of oxytocin, leading to more collaboration and connection.

Research from Syracuse University finds that falling in love takes a fifth of a second. It's more a function of intuition than intention and rational analysis. Love stimulates euphoria and intelligence that characterizes the magic in that fifth of a second.

What happens before and after depends entirely on the quality of our conversations.

What strengths do or could you bring to emotional intimacy with another?

How would connecting conversations add to the quality of emotional intimacy?

Reflection
Practice

Take time to invite more connecting conversations with the people you feel are most important to you, whether you talk with them often or not enough.

In even brief touching or hugging, have your intention be less about the symbolism than having it be a way of being present to another's energy.

# Conversational Freedom

In the study for this book, 92% of participants reported that conversational freedom is intrinsic to connecting conversations. We grow a sense of trust strong enough for people to feel free to talk about anything.

It's interesting how much freedom we give ourselves and each other in conversations. The more freedom we have to explore and share new things, the more interesting our potential for fluency and connection.

It's easy to get into patterns with people. We have certain kinds of conversations with certain people. We find ourselves talking about only certain kinds of things with our intimate others, our children and parents, our families and friends, coworkers and bosses, neighbors and strangers. Whether these are more comfortable or uncomfortable patterns, they are still patterns that become connection-limiting.

We have more connecting conversations when we invite and engage in a fuller range of things. If moving into one new territory doesn't work, we can try other territories. We can't assume historical patterns are destiny.

What are your patterns of talking about the same kinds of things to the same people?

If you gave yourself more freedom to talk about anything to anyone, what you want to feel free to talk about?

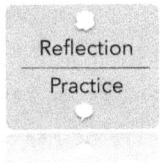

Reflection
Practice

In your next few conversations, ask or talk about something potentially relevant to both of you that you don't normally talk or ask about with them.

Think of things you'd like to learn about and invite conversations with people you know or know about to learn with them.

# Mindful Conversations

In her groundbreaking mindfulness research at Harvard, Ellen Langer talks about mindfulness as being fully present and engaged in noticing anything new in our world.

Presence is curiosity. Curiosity is consciousness. The more conscious we are the more capable we become of connecting conversations.

Connecting conversations are mindful conversations because we are always seeking to discover, notice and learn something new about each other. The trust we feel together directly radiates from the way we are mindfully together in conversation. Our mutual interest in each other informs and inspires discovery of new things about each other. Each conversation is fresh rather than stale, rehashed or mindlessly habitual.

When we are present, we are naturally less attached to expectations and emotions. The conversation can be rich in both and none get in the way of our connectedness, and in fact provide grist for the connectedness mill. Mindfulness animates banter, calms tense and focuses utility conversations.

In what kinds of conversations do you feel most and least present?

What assumptions do you make about people you have the most regular conversations related to what you think is and isn't changing in their lives?

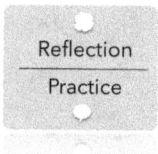

Reflection
Practice

In any conversation, notice the subtle and obvious shifts in people's voice, posture, attentiveness, emotions and interests.

Ask people how their world is in any way different this week than last week, last month or last year.

# Conversation Hacks

# The Pattern Language of Bad Conversations

The pattern languages of bad conversations are deflections and denials. Defections are opposites of flow; denials are opposites of sync.

Deflections happen in self-interest and unresponsiveness. In self-interest, we use the time together to draw attention to anything about ourselves. We feel free to show little or no interest in others in the conversation. Others should feel fulfilled listening, enjoying, agreeing and supplying supporting material from their experience.

We are unresponsive when, after someone says something, we go on to talking about something not exactly or largely not relevant to what was said, or we talk to or at someone else. We neither validate nor invalidate what they just said. People feel unheard or unsure of being heard.

Denials happen in invalidation and inconsolability. Invalidation is reacting immediately with disagreement, pushback, fault finding or contrarian positions. Whether it comes from data or opinion, it comes across as righteous refusal of what is said. Inconsolability is refusing empathy, support or help. We argue that nothing anyone else offers helps, has value or is appreciated.

The good news about deflection and denial is how easy the connecting alternatives are. It takes roughly the same amount of time to be validating, grateful, interested and relevant as deflecting and denying.

In what kinds of conversations do you think it is vital to avoid any form of defection or denial, and why?

What are the advantages of instead helping people feel validated, appreciated, attended to and engaged?

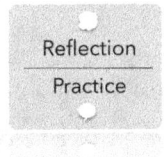

Reflection
Practice

When anticipating any tense conversation explore what the alternatives to deflection and denial might sound like.

Think of other ways you could avoid contributing to bad conversations.

## Distancing

It's interesting to think of connection as our natural relationship to others. We feel naturally connected to others to the extent that none of us does any kind of distancing. We actually have to do distancing to miss or lose the connection.

Distancing happens internally as we tell ourselves the story that we have little or nothing in common with others. It happens externally as we use unfamiliar language and references.

We insert negative judgment or suspicion. We challenge what others say. We ignore what other ask. We go on after another speaks as if they said nothing of importance or relevance to us. We text too much.

No one who does distancing is even aware they are. They stay unconscious of simple signals of disconnection. We keep the distance our secret held closely or shared with intimate others.

Of the more subtle kinds of distancing in conversations are the kinds of superficial friendliness, politeness or role correctness we express in banter, utility, tense and awkward conversations. Each is pleasant or expedient and not emotionally connecting.

Just knowing this allows us to be more conscious of not distancing and instead realizing our intrinsic connectedness to others.

How might you use language, references or conversational topics others would not easily relate to?

What would it mean to pay more attention to similarities between you and others you share conversations with?

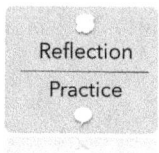

Monitor yourself to notice any signs of even subtle criticism or other forms of distancing.

Make a point in any conversation to explicitly acknowledge how you and other are similar.

## Landmines

We live in a world where some of us continue to value hostile conversations. We patronize all manner of media that invest billions of dollars daily to be the echo chambers of choice for those of us personally dedicated to hostile conversations, conversations of division. We would reject out of hand an invitation to a connecting conversation by one of "them."

Conversational landmines are potentially sensitive and volatile topics that can create social risks and costs that exceed benefits. Politics and religion are classic landmine possibilities when we're in conversation with people whose beliefs and biases are at odds.

The convenient strategy is denial, refusing to engage in any potentially divisive topic or question, pretending to act as if differences don't exist.

The social cost to this strategy is that we don't grow in our learning and deeper understanding of the polarities. As long as we resist, we make it more possible for us to become more learning-disabled when it comes to the topics. In the worst cases, we constrain ourselves to conversations that only strengthen our learning disabilities.

Whole societies can fail to progress in the way they live out their politics and religions when people fail to host and invite connecting conversations around them. Polarization continues and we squander opportunities to connect more deeply.

Political and religious differences can be rich opportunity spaces for mutual curiosity and learning more about each other, and ourselves.

These difference are often ripe opportunities for mutual interest because many religious and political positions are generalizations.

We can inquire into the specifics of what each of us actually knows, feels and wants. We don't have to resort to tense conversations, thrashing against each other's differences.

We can talk about the origins of our own positions. We can share and inquire about the people who originally exposed us to our political and religious paths, what they were like then and how we are today like and unlike them. We can share the kinds of questions we would ask our favorite current political and religious leaders and how we would answer those.

We can talk about the enemies of our positions and what we think their growing up was, or must have been like.

We can talk about our loves, the people we think are adding unique or amazing value to our world and what we most appreciate about them.

Shared curiosity improves our chances for genuine discovery and compassion. It's the only way the world will heal divisions that devastate the lives of millions of innocent and fragile children and their mothers and grandmothers every day.

The next time you're in a somewhat to more intense political or religious conversation, how would you ideally like to feel in that conversation?

What could help people in politically or religiously polarized conversations better listen?

Reflection
Practice

In conversations of political or religious differences, ask people if they have always had exactly the same positions and if they have shifted or become more complex or nuanced over time.

When people talk about political or religious positions or events, be interested in how those make them feel and how these positions show up in their everyday life.

## Personas

In connecting conversations, we look and listen beyond our personas. Personas are the images we have of each other, often based on the assumptions of roles, status, stereotypes, stories and history.

In connecting conversations, we're interacting with people as they are rather than their personas. We see that our parents and children are like no other parents and children. Our friends and colleagues are like no others. Our neighbors and strangers are like no others. We notice how each differs from our expectation of how they should be.

We see and listen beyond the assumptions of generalizations. We show up so transparent others see us in our uniqueness, not as images crafted from their assumptions.

We assume certain things about people because they are our spouses or partners, parents or children, siblings or friends, bosses or coworkers, neighbors or strangers. We have assumptions based on how people look, talk and interact. We make assumptions based on gender and generation.

One of the signals we're interacting with personas is treating interpretation as fact. This can come out as "So obviously what you're saying is ..." about what clearly wasn't explicitly expressed. Interacting with someone's persona makes connecting conversations less possible.

In connecting conversations we instead translate all assumptions, even our most cherished, into questions for exploration and deeper listening. We like when people feel accurately heard and known.

How do your assumptions about the interests of others play into especially tense and awkward conversations?

What would your conversations be like if you translated every assumption about others into questions?

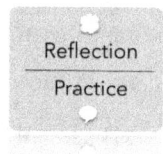

Reflection
Practice

In any upcoming conversation, monitor your inner monologue for any kinds of assumptions you're making about others.

Ask others question to explore any exceptions to your assumptions about them.

## Personalities

Each of us has a unique chemistry of default relational habits. We are more naturally funny or worried, talkers or listeners, planners or spontaneous, perfectionists or pragmatists, compassionate or critical, change loving or adverse, analytical or creative, analog or digital, daring or cautious, past or future oriented, urban or suburban, xenophobes or xenophiles, text or talk.

Although we have more practice with one side of any personality pair, each of us has the potential for both sides of every personality coin.

We can ask for stories that reveal both and in most cases find people have stories about both, even though in each pairing, one can be more the natural default.

It is our capacity for both-and that gives us resilience, adaptability and agility in this world of unprecedented change, uncertainty and connectivity.

In connecting conversations, we honor our wholeness, our capacity for both. We stay interested in how we are both-and rather than either-or. To the extent that we are interested in each other's wholeness, we can be connected.

The more we discover and appreciate the wholeness of others, the more we get clear on the value of our wholeness.

What happens when you're in a conversation with someone you've labeled as being a certain personality type?

What would conversations be like if you acknowledged that everyone has the potential for both sides of any personality pair?

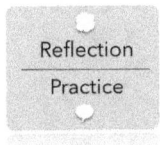

Reflection
Practice

Explore with people about how they have experienced and expressed the personalities that we experience as the less dominant side of the pair, getting examples and stories.

Share examples and stories of your own experience in both sides of personality pairs.

# Diffusers and Escalators

In tense conversations, we can diffuse or escalate the emotional weather and climate.

On the diffuse side of the equation we have humor, banter, expressions of appreciation and empathy and of course moving into more of a connecting conversation.

On the escalate side we have invalidating the reality of others, claiming others aren't listening or understanding, using examples to further illustrate what others are already defensive about, making threats of any kind and shutting people out.

Unlike connecting conversations, sensitivities are magnified in tense conversations. Anything and everything said and done has the potential to diffuse or escalate emotions and sense of connection or disconnection. The smallest looks or gestures, choices of words, tones matter.

In every conversation there is a whole dialogue between our energy fields that takes place below our conscious awareness, the whole time acting like an invisible hand shaping how the whole conversation feels and forms. The more self-aware we stay in conversations, the more we can monitor and adjust our energy.

The more quiet our energy, the easier it is for others to hear and understand us, hear and speak their truth kindly and entertain new possibilities. Keeping our energy quiet means staying present, aware of the physical and temporal spaces between words, between us and around us.

Being positive in anything works. Researchers Judith and Richard Glaser talk about how brain chemistry plays into conversational intelligence, our ability to think creatively, empathetically and strategically with others.

Critical actions and words that raise cortisol levels cause us to be overly sensitive and reactive. Higher cortisol levels shut down the thinking centers in our brain as we go into protective mode. These effects can last more than 24 hours. With rumination and more conversation about criticisms, we can extend and imprint the effects.

Positive words and actions produce oxytocin that activates our prefrontal cortex involved in trusting thinking and communication. Because oxytocin metabolizes more quickly than cortisol, its effects are less long lasting and must be restimulated by positivity. The more oxytocin we create, the higher our conversational intelligence becomes.

Researcher Paul Zak points out that just observing someone suffer releases oxytocin, which leads to more empathy and generosity with strangers. This has direct implication in organizations and relationships of all kinds. Oxytocin is high when we're connected. We stay focused, trusting and productive.

What are your more common ways to diffuse and escalate tense conversations?

What could make you more present in tense conversations?

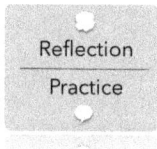

In tense conversations, think of ways to express more empathy for what others feel.

Consider any ways to lighten up serious and heavy conversations, even a bit.

# Soft No

We each have people in our lives who sometimes, or too often, ask too much of us. Out of a sense of neediness, entitlement, role expectation, agreement or dependency on our generosity, they expect more than what we can currently deliver.

A hard no us just that. No, period. No excuses, apologies, promises or alternatives. A soft no offers some or all of these. It's less distancing, more caring. The hard no doesn't care; the soft no cares.

The soft no invites problem solving and exploration of alternatives including conditional postponements: "I could say yes to that if …"

Whether we get a hard or soft no from others, simple factors like the quality of verbal expression matters. University of Michigan's Jose Benki, studied 1380 total calls made by a hundred interviewers for telephone surveys.

He wanted to see which interviewers were most successful at getting respondents to agree with the survey by providing a "yes" answer to the questions. He finds that a moderate conversational speed of 3.5 words per second rather than very fast or slow garners more yeses.

It's the subtle things that can turn hard no into soft no, and yes.

What are situations when a soft rather than hard no would make for more connecting conversations?

When are we more likely to say yes when we really mean no?

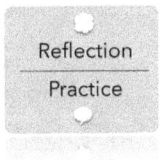

Reflection
Practice

When preparing to deliver a no, practice the art of yes-if.

When delivering a no, give others as much context as possible for your decision and offer alternatives whenever possible.

## Conversation As Invitation

An invitation is a welcoming space of choice. The invited feel genuinely free to accept, decline or defer. They feel comfortable engaging as much or little as they like.

When we initiate conversation as invitation instead of imposition we pay attention to how much it feels like the invited want to talk. When it feels like they would like some space, we give them the space they need.

One word answers to our questions and lack of interest in our experience can signal preference for space. How friendly people seem is not always a reliable indicator they intend connection or space.

It is an act of kindness to invite anyone into conversation. Our invitation makes it more possible for them to feel like they exist, they matter, they are not alone on their path, someone cares about what they know, feel and want, they live on a planet abundant with good people.

Each of us has our own baseline desire for conversation. Some of us are typically on the higher end and others on the lower end. We all have exceptions where higher end people have times of wanting to speak to no one and lower end people have times of wanting to speak to others.

When we invite a conversation and easily realize another seeks space, we can kindly help create a gracious exit for them, or us. For us, we can say what we were just about to do. For them, we can ask where they're off to next.

What for you are the subtle and obvious signals that people do and don't want a conversation?

How do you signal others that you do or don't seek a conversation?

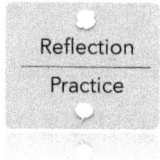

Reflection
Practice

Resist postponing a conversation invitation on the basis that you don't know if others do or don't want one.

Give others gracious exits from conversation invitations they seem to decline as soon as the signals are clear.

# Before You Die

More often than we might like, we have to say last goodbyes. If we get enough of a head start, we can say and ask everything we think we want to say and ask, until we later remember other things time did not permit.

It is an unreasonable expectation that we will ever have the time we need or want to finish unfinished business or express fully the depths of mutual gratitude. Each last conversation humbly offers an invitation to the gift of connection.

These can be incredibly beautiful connecting conversations, even about the amazing experience of passing, if others have the cognition and expressive capacities for it. In our most lucid and present moments, we can share moment to moment unfolding exploration of every nuance of the space.

There is nothing intrinsically about last goodbyes that require them to be awkward, tense or banter. They can be magnificently connecting.

We can continue in and leave this world with yet more new insights into the thin consciousness membrane between the visited known and vast unknown.

How could our last conversations with anyone who matters to us be beautiful conversations?

What would we postpone saying to anyone close to us and what would make it more possible for us to say these things now?

Reflection
Practice

Think of three people you care most about and consider what you'd want them to know before your last conversation with them.

Invite an intentionally connecting conversation with the oldest person you know.

## Inspiring Compassion

Sometimes our conversational interest is to inspire more compassion in others. In our enduring dedication to their happiness and wellbeing, we wish understanding for them where they struggle without it.

Researcher Paul Slovic and his team study compassion fade. This is the reality that if people are asked to donate to one person in need, they will more likely do so than they would if asked to donate to two or more.

The more people we are asked to donate to, the more we are ironically desensitized to the need.

Compassion is appealing to another's ability to relate to someone else's struggle or suffering.

Modeling, inviting and inspiring compassion through stories and anecdotes helps others move from feeling irritated, frustrated or angry to more of a space of compassion. It nurtures immediate and sustained emotional connection.

This is motivation enough for us to be vigorous story collectors and tellers of narratives about people who struggle in all walks of life. We can discover and share all kinds of stories about those whose narratives can become new sources of compassion.

Who in your life and world can struggle with compassion and how can it be a struggle for you?

How does compassion not lower our standards or violate our principles?

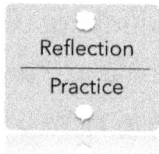

Reflection
Practice

Take anything you might want to have more compassion about and research more stories about it.

Take more time to express and describe your own compassion in conversations where others might be struggling with it.

# Social Responsibility

In connection, we act with more caring, creativity and courage. In disconnection, we are more self-absorbed, rigid and cautious. Relationships are easier and richer in connection. This means intimate, friend, family, work, community and stranger relationships.

Not being connected leads to isolation, tension, depression, addiction and violence. Everything we try to legislate and go to war against is a function of disconnection.

We will see the quality of relationships of all kinds on the planet grow to the extent that we all learn how to have more connecting conversations.

Having more technical access to each other apparently doesn't always equate to more quality connections.

We will see generosity and compassion increase and isolation and violence decrease when people learn how to have connecting conversations with others they know and don't know. Imagine if every gun, drug, act of bullying and denial of rights were replaced by countless connecting conversations.

We now have growing empirical evidence that the array of social costs of addiction, educational failure, unemployment, homelessness and violence have at root social disconnection.

At root to social disconnection is a lack of capacity for connecting conversations. This is not to say that people struggling with social costs lack conversations. They can have lives packed with toxic and disconnecting conversations.

On the opposite end of the social spectrum, we have people living flourishing lives of wellbeing and engagement. Intrinsic to their experience is capacity for social connection. They seek and sustain connecting conversations.

Conversational poverty is the ultimate poverty of spirit and the most profound source of deep disconnection. Every connecting conversation is a personal, spiritual and socially responsible act.

How does it make sense that underneath any social problem is social isolation, the debilitating lack of connecting conversations?

How could toxic personal conversations lead to social costs that public policy doesn't seem able to influence?

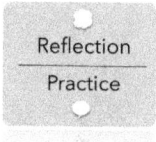

Make a point to bring the more quiet and reserved people in your life or work into conversations.

Invite banter conversations with strangers in public and common spaces.

# Conversation Everyday

# New Conversations

New conversations have their own beauty.

**We have new things to share.**

We take time to learn new things about our interests and our world. We use them to start and refresh new conversations with people familiar and unfamiliar to us. We use them to weave longer and richer conversations. If we follow and friend interesting people on social media, there is no shortage of new possibilities for learning, exploring and sharing.

All of this happens through the intentionality of having new questions for our quests and the serendipity of stumbling on gems of insight.

**We have new people in our conversations.**

New people bring new sets of stories, reports, questions, language and perspectives. They enlarge and sometimes challenge our felt rightness of views.

We don't have to just invite one or two new people in conversations. We can invite several different people. Variety matters. The more people bring what we don't, the more possibilities there are for new conversations. They can be from other kinds of work, interests, cultures, generations, faith and political perspectives.

**We can talk in new places.**

Each change in conversational venue opens up opportunities for new conversations. It can be in nature, at the beach, in museums and galleries, coffee shops, restaurants and pubs. Walking conversations shift the energy to new options for chatting and exploring.

What opportunities do you have these days to invite and shape any kinds of new conversations?

How could you improvise with new ways of inviting new conversations in your life and work?

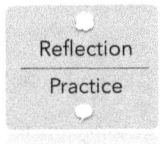

Reflection
Practice

Populate your calendar with plans for new conversations, with new people, in new places.

Invite people who don't yet know each other, both of whom you like, into any kind of new conversation.

## At Work

There are endless places to insert connecting conversations at work. They uniquely create and grow trust in ways that banter and utility conversations often don't.

They are ideal when people join or leave a team, when new leaders are introduced and when we're bonding with clients, customers and partners. They serve us well when we're waiting for and starting meetings. They are welcome when we're moving into and through tense conversations.

We use connecting conversations when we're introducing people for new collaborations and projects. We keep virtual teams and relationships strong and growing with connecting conversations.

The more we invite connecting conversations and make them normative, the more free people feel to have them.

The fragmentation, isolation and division we see among people and teams is often simply the lack of connecting conversations, a problem easily remedied with new learning experiences. The symptomatic trends of low morale, bad turnover, weak and toxic leadership, lack of focus and attention and misalignments are all reflections on the quality of conversations in organizations.

The more we help people learn how to invite and engage in connecting conversations, the more possible they become. They come about through practice not policy.

Why can informal conversations be more connecting and productive than formal?

Why is it that the quality of our conversations has such an significant impact on everything that happens well and not well at work?

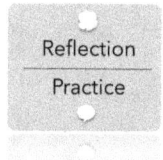

Reflection
Practice

Invite people into more informal conversations when time is available and you want to grow existing or new connections with people at work.

Invite people with whom you would like to connect with more into a conversation so they can discover possible mutual helping and collaboration possibilities.

## Agendas

Depending on our relationship to uncertainty, we prefer imposed or improvised agendas in the utility conversations we call meetings.

People with low tolerance for uncertainty prefer preset, enforced agendas. A timed agenda is even better because it makes predictability that much more possible.

The agenda lovers' narrative is that all manner of meeting ills emanate from the lack of tightly managed agendas. Their experience has been dominated by bad, unstructured meetings squandered by banter, awkward and tense rather than productive utility conversations.

People who view uncertainty as a space of possibilities rather than risks like meetings with the agile flexibility of emerging agendas. In emerging agendas, anyone can invite a new or continuing conversation.

We can start formal or informal meetings asking who wants to start or continue a conversation. We can ask who wants to contribute to any and decide together for the time we have, which ones it makes sense to have. We take any unfinished conversation beyond the meeting.

In some cases, it makes sense to have multiple concurrent conversations because not everyone want or needs to be in all of them. This practice optimizes the quality of conversations because in high quality conversations, there are more turns taken per hour. The worst scenario is a table or room full of people disengaged in listening to others talk.

People who value uncertainty believe that the serendipity of unstructured water cooler, hallway and happy hour conversations can be at least if not more productive and connecting than imposed agenda conversations.

Preset agendas form conversational boundaries. They define what people should feel invited and not invited to talk or inquire. Conversations with emerging agendas make everyone feel invited to engage.

With the ever-growing field of communication and collaboration applications, any number of inclusive and productive conversations can begin and complete in real time.

Connecting conversations don't have imposed agendas because they don't have intentional boundaries. We are free to talk about whatever we feel would be most productive and connecting. Everyone feels heard, understood, valued and engaged.

As more people learn how to have connecting conversations, mutual interest makes for the best conversations possible, without presumptive agendas. Nothing in connecting conversations is presumptive. Everyone is a conversation inviter. No one dominates what we all engage in together.

One of the indicators that people are getting better at connecting conversations is that when they do suggest or invite agendas, they shape them as questions rather than topics. This naturally and immediately sets the tone for a more connecting space.

How can imposed agendas make some people feel disengaged, less important?

Why would agendas as questions have more power to engage than agendas as topics?

In an upcoming meeting suggest that participants co-create the agenda before or at the beginning of the meeting.

Make any scheduled meeting look and feel more like connecting conversations.

## Side Conversations

Depending on the situation, side conversations can create more connecting conversations. Structurally, they allow for more turn taking than a single conversion in a group.

One dynamic is the culture of the group. In formal and awkward contexts, side conversations can be seen as impolite or rude. There is at least an implicit expectation of one person talking at a time and usually in these contexts, interruptions are unwelcome.

Side conversations can be interpreted as disinterest in the singular dominating speaker. In work and public settings, the hosts might actually impose or suggest a rule about singular dominant speaking.

In informal contexts, side conversations can create more connecting conversations, especially when singular dominant speaking keeps the conversation more disengaging.

In larger groups, people can flow in and out of connecting side conversations. It's possible to cultivate the fine art of being in side conversations while staying present to the periphery of other opportunities. We can also optimize the engagement of others by connecting people and dots across side conversations.

When we host group conversations, we can implicitly and explicitly encourage side conversations and engage in any to help make them as connecting as possible.

What is the potential power of side conversations?

How can you help create a conversational environment informal enough for people to have side conversations?

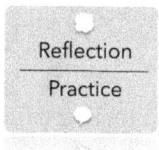

When you're in a group of four or more, and the tone supports it, invite side conversations to enliven and enrich the energy.

When leading meetings of any kind, encourage side conversations as long as time is given for people to later share relevant conclusions.

## Growing Ideas

Some conversations are about growing new ideas, particularly in utility and tense conversations.

New ideas don't grow by discussing proposals. They grow in very specifically nurturing conversational environments. There are five idea nutrients: *like, so, and, when* and *else*.

*Like* is what we like about any idea that emerges. "What do we like about this idea?" Every idea has some potential upsides, even when the costs and downsides would consider the idea in its current form untenable. Acknowledging likes allows us to make sure the potential value of any idea inspires and informs next possibilities.

*So* is a question for more details on an idea. "So can you tell me more about how you see …?" Ideas with more details become more coherent and potentially useful moving forward. Details become inspiration for alternative considerations that grow ideas.

*And* is what could make an idea stronger. "And, we could also include …" We propose new features that could make an idea more useful and attractive and less costly to produce and use.

*When* is the timing of ideas. The most vital characteristic of successful ideas is that they are well-timed. "When could this idea happen, given what needs to come before?" We talk about what we might need to happen before this idea could be best possible. We talk about what factors would indicate the best timing for this idea. We move from *whether* to *when*.

*Else* is another way to achieve the same benefits of an idea. "How else could we realize the advantages and minimize the disadvantages of this idea?" This is the simple groundbreaking invention of Kleenex to do the job of handkerchiefs without a pocket germ incubator.

The most significant impact of the idea nutrients is how they build trust between and among us. New ideas grow at the speed of trust.

Which of the five idea growing nutrients do you already use on a regular basis when growing ideas with others?

What would be idea toxins that would prevent the growth of ideas together?

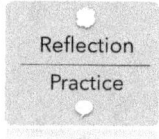

Reflection

Practice

The next time you're in a group seeking to grow new ideas, introduce any of the five idea growing nutrients and invite others to do the same through questions to them.

Respond to virtual idea proposals with the five nutrients.

# Talk To Action

One of the most salient aspects of connecting conversations is how they naturally and intuitively lead to action.

When we feel connected, we are more prone to investing time in what matters. We talk about what matters and our lives more specifically reflect in action what matters most to us. We do together what neither and none of us could do alone, in isolation or opposition.

Certainly utility conversations ideally lead to action and tense conversations gone well result in action. Agreements are actions. It is unrealistic to expect banter or awkward conversations to spark action. Connecting conversations have the greatest potential for shared, meaningful action.

What kinds of conversations do you wish would lead to action more often and easily?

What needs to happen for anyone to move from talk to action, even in connecting conversations?

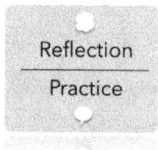

Reflection
Practice

When you want action from a conversation, invite it, clearly and unapologetically.

Take initiative to be the first to commit to action from a conversation.

# In Community

We think communities of disconnection and division are so because of the basic political, social, economic, cultural and educational differences there.

As real as these are, and as much they are scapegoated for tensions and costs, they do not define the essential differences between floundering and flourishing communities.

It doesn't take advanced degrees in anthropology to realize that the quality of life in communities reflects the quality of conversations there.

Flourishing and floundering communities have dramatically different kinds of conversations that dominate their contrasting cultures. The conversations of floundering communities create, grow and sustain disconnection and division. The conversations of flourishing communities create, grow and sustain connection and alignment.

In floundering communities, people talk predominantly about problems, deficiencies and blame. Flourishing communities talk about dreams, assets, commitments and invitations. Foundering communities talk about gossip that divides. Flourishing communities talk about stories that inspire.

Anyone can shape and shift conversations as they unfold and intersect at kitchen tables, porches, coffee shops, happy hours, religious gatherings and public meetings. Formal and informal leaders have unique opportunities to host and invite new conversations that connect people in the growing of flourishing cultures.

There are many simple, possible connecting conversations in communities. What would we most love to see possible? What talents and resources do we have available to realize these possibilities? What can we do right now to leverage these assets toward these dreams? Who else should we invite to these conversations?

Each question creates the kind of connecting trust that makes creativity and collaboration more possible than ever.

Considering things in your community you most value, what do you imagine were the kinds of conversations that launched their beginnings?

When you have conversations about your neighborhood or regional communities, are they more floundering or flourishing conversations?

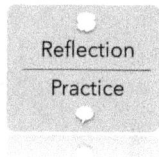

Reflection
Practice

Any time you're in a floundering conversation with people about their communities, do anything to shift it to a more flourishing conversation.

When you find people who love where they live, ask them specifically what stories are on their lists of likes and loves.

## Intentional Conversations

It's natural to allow our conversations to be shaped by the gravitational pull of the emotional weather or climate.

It's natural to have tense conversations when we feel tensions, utility conversations when we feel urgencies and banter conversations when we feel relaxed.

In intentional conversations, we have the conversations we want to have, however we feel.

We can have hilarious conversations at formal meetings and crashing exhausted on couches, serous conversations at parties and bars and connecting conversations anywhere. We can have feelings follow conversations rather than conversations follow feelings.

This invites more conversational freedom. We are less constrained by our moods and the moods of others. We can invite what we want to feel together rather than feel obligated by how we feel.

Instead of just asking people how they feel, we ask how they want to feel and invite the kinds of conversations that would most easily get us there.

What we talk about together any at point in time does not need to be determined by moods, current events or habits. Any season can be a good season to have beautiful connecting conversations.

How intentional would you want to be in your everyday conversations?

What would your life be like if it was shaped by more intentional conversations?

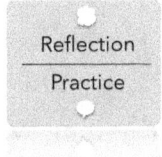

Reflection
Practice

Experiment with inviting intentional conversations, especially with people whose can be more mood or event driven.

Start more conversations with an invitation of "Would you like to talk about ...?" and suggest questions that could inspire how you want to intentionally feel together.

# Rich Time Together

There are so many ways to have rich time together. This is time in connecting conversations inspired by rich experiences.

We can share a film, a book, a museum or art gallery visit, a volunteer experience, travel, a talk, meditation or yoga together. We can attend concerts, theater or poetry and storytelling events. We can join each other in events that represent interests we don't have in common, stretching our conversational boundaries.

Each offers a unique way to discover more about each other, to practice the mutual interest in connecting conversations.

Thinking of people with whom you want to have more connecting conversations, what are potentially interesting things you've never done together?

What interests of yours could you share with others you have never before?

Reflection

Practice

With someone you want to deepen a connection, spend time sharing new rich experience possibilities.

Trade appreciative kidnappings, where one of you plans and takes the other or others to a surprise experience everyone might enjoy, with generous conversations following.

# Walking Conversations

There is a certain magic in walking conversations. The rhythm of walking creates a clear, calm mind providing the ideal environment for connecting conversations as well as banter and tense conversations.

Walking together makes eye contact easier, especially for people sensitive to too much closeness through eye contact and when tense conversations make eye contact uncomfortable.

The shared sense experience creates a sense of a common world. This inspires our potential for connection.

Stanford research indicates that walking boosts creativity by 81%, which benefits connecting conversations that thrive on creativity in our questions of interest in each other. It also tells us that walking in natural settings lowers anxiety and brooding, increasing happiness, which adds richness to connecting conversations. This is good news for tense and awkward conversations.

What were some of your best walking conversations like?

When would walking conversations be valuable with others you know and with whom you want to get more connected?

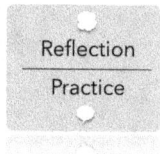

Reflection
Practice

Schedule a walking conversation with someone with whom you want to transition from banter, tense or awkward to more connecting conversations.

Explore new walking venues especially in nature for future walking conversations.

# Talk With Anyone, About Anything

Our life is infinitely richer when we cultivate the art of being able with talk to anyone about anything. This is feeling not only comfortable, but energized talking with people who look, think or live similarly or differently across genders, generations and geographies.

It starts with questioning assumptions about how impossibly different others are.

From the 1% who own most of the world's wealth and don't have to work because their money works for them to the 2 billion who live on less than $2 a day and toil hard for access to water, food, dignity and medicine, every one of the seven plus billion people on the planet bring to every conversation the gifts of stories, wishes, struggles and questions. Many of these have themes we share.

We can inquire and share about any of this. We can offer a compliment or wish for them. We can ask for their feedback, advice or help. We can talk about news and weather and anything we see or hear in common around us. We can grow trust by validating the truth of their experience.

We can avoid things that get in the way like getting personal too quickly, making everything about us, offering unsolicited criticism, one-upping their stories, dominating and showing interest only in what they talk about rather than in them personally.

We can talk with anyone about their day and week, their hopes for what's next in their life. We can talk about anyone and anything they and we care about. We can share stories with lessons and messages any human being can relate to. The possibilities are endless.

It doesn't matter that someone represents a generation or ethnicity, background or way of life about which we have little exposure. It doesn't matter how much we tell ourselves the story they have nothing in common with us or those we like and love.

The earth belongs to the heart inspired by endless passion for learning. As long as we can show up interested in what others know, feel and want, we can talk with anyone about anything. We can connect and flourish together in the art of conversations.

Who are strangers in the past with whom you've had some of the most unlikely conversations and what did you do to help make those happen?

What are things you have in common with billions of other people on the planet, thinking specifically in terms of struggles, stories, wishes, questions and dreams?

Reflection
Practice

Imagine being with the most unlikely nice person on the planet you'd ever meet and imagine different ways you could begin a conversation.

At the next event you attend, start no less than five conversations with people you don't know well.

# Looking Up At The Moon

When we connect with each other, we connect with a space beyond the known. In the awe of mutual curiosity, we feel connected to spaces larger than ourselves.

We discover each other in new ways. In discovering each other, we find deeper connections to ourselves. Through the eyes of each other, we more deeply glimpse into the mystery that we are.

Each of us is a galaxy of unknowns yet to be discovered. Each connecting conversation is a magical space of gazing together into the deep starry sky of wonder, delighted companions, looking up at the moon.

# Gratitude

Many thanks to Jen Margolis for inspiring the Reflections and Practice sections, to Brett Joseph for helping shape the global study and Sandy Halem for her expert insights into the art of dialogue.

Thanks to the countless researchers from around the world who have shared with us the ever amazing science of connections. Thanks to my family, mentors, colleagues and friends who have opened our hearts to the possibilities of conversations.

# Jack Ricchiuto

Jack is a writer whose research, facilitation and coaching focuses on helping people grow deeper connections in their organizations and communities. He is the originator of the The Agile Canvas that is globally revolutionizing the way we grow smart organizations.

20-time author, Jack has been delivering workshops and coaching over the past 3 decades, in over 24 industry sectors with hundreds of organizations and dozens of communities across the US and globally. Jack's work is based on his experience, his writing and the latest science and research.

Jack has worked with multi-national companies, foundations and non-profits like IBM, PayPal, NASA, American Red Cross, Smucker's, FedEx, Federal

Reserve Bank, USDA, Switzer Foundation, E&Y and investment leaders from Silicon Valley. He is a managing partner with Thrive@Work.

Jack has taught in graduate and post-graduate programs in the areas of positive leadership, community building, entrepreneurship and storytelling including at Harvard Kennedy Business School, UC Berkeley, Vanderbilt, Tecnologico de Monterrey and Kent State University's EMBA program. He was one of the first virtual collaboration designers, bloggers, social media and social network experts.

Jack's 20 books include *Collaborative Creativity, Accidental Conversations, Project Zen, Appreciative Leadership, Mountain Paths, Conscious Becoming, Instructions from the Cook, The Stories that Connect Us, The Enchantment of Casual Origins, The Joy of Thriving, Ordinary Eyes, The Agile Canvas Field*

*Guide, Abundant Possibilities, The Power Of Circles, Making Sense Of Time, Beyond Recipes, Focus, Smarter Together, Ideas* and *The Art Of Conversations.*

With a graduate degree in positive psychology from Goddard College, Jack was trained by global leaders in American, European and Japanese transformation models. Jack continues to coach entrepreneurs and intrapreneurs as he has since the late 90s.

For more about the book, the author and workshops, visit TheArtOfConversations.com